1935 if read a good book, you needed either a lot of money or a library card. Cheap paperbacks were available, but their poor production generally mirrored the quality between the covers. One weekend that year, Allen Lane, Managing Director of The Bodley Head, having spent the weekend visiting Agatha Christie, found himself on a platform at Exeter station trying to find something to read for his journey back to London. He was appalled by the quality of the material he had to choose from. Everything that Allen Lane achieved from that day until his death in 1970 was based on a passionate belief in the existence of 'a vast reading public for *intelligent* books at a low price'. The result of his momentous vision was the birth not only of Penguin, but of the 'paperback revolution'. Quality writing became available for the price of a packet of cigarettes, literature became a mass medium for the first time, a nation of book-borrowers became a nation of book-buyers – and the very concept of book publishing was changed for ever. Those founding principles – of quality and value, with an overarching belief in the fundamental importance of reading – have guided everything the company has done since 1935. Sir Allen Lane's pioneering spirit is still very much alive at Penguin in 2005. Here's to the next 70 years!

MORE THAN A BUSINESS

'We decided it was time to end the almost customary half-hearted manner in which cheap editions were produced – as though the only people who could possibly want cheap editions must belong to a lower order of intelligence. We, however, believed in the existence in this country of a vast reading public for intelligent books at a low price, and staked everything on it'
Sir Allen Lane, 1902–1970

'The Penguin Books are splendid value for sixpence, so splendid that if other publishers had any sense they would combine against them and suppress them'
George Orwell

'More than a business … a national cultural asset'
Guardian

'When you look at the whole Penguin achievement you know that it constitutes, in action, one of the more democratic successes of our recent social history'
Richard Hoggart

The Desert and the Dancing Girls

GUSTAVE FLAUBERT

PENGUIN BOOKS

PENGUIN BOOKS

Published by the Penguin Group
Penguin Books Ltd, 80 Strand, London WC2R ORL, England
Penguin Group (USA) Inc., 375 Hudson Street, New York, New York 10014, USA
Penguin Group (Canada), 10 Alcorn Avenue, Toronto, Ontario, Canada M4V 3B2
(a division of Pearson Penguin Canada Inc.)
Penguin Ireland, 25 St Stephen's Green, Dublin 2, Ireland
(a division of Penguin Books Ltd)
Penguin Group (Australia), 250 Camberwell Road, Camberwell, Victoria 3124,
Australia (a division of Pearson Australia Group Pty Ltd)
Penguin Books India Pvt Ltd, 11 Community Centre,
Panchsheel Park, New Delhi – 110 017, India
Penguin Group (NZ), cnr Airborne and Rosedale Roads, Albany,
Auckland 1310, New Zealand (a division of Pearson New Zealand Ltd)
Penguin Books (South Africa) (Pty) Ltd, 24 Sturdee Avenue,
Rosebank 2196, South Africa

Penguin Books Ltd, Registered Offices: 80 Strand, London WC2R ORL, England

www.penguin.com

Flaubert in Egypt first published in the
USA by Academy Chicago Publishers 1979
Published in Penguin Books 1996
This extract published as a Pocket Penguin 2005

1

Translation copyright © Francis Steegmuller, 1972
All rights reserved

Set in 11.5/13.5pt Monotype Dante
Typeset by Palimpsest Book Production Limited
Polmont, Stirlingshire
Printed in England by Clays Ltd, St Ives plc

Flaubert to His Mother

. . . When we were two hours out from the coast of Egypt I went into the bow with the chief quartermaster and saw the seraglio of Abbas Pasha like a black dome on the blue of the Mediterranean. The sun was beating down on it. I had my first sight of the Orient through, or rather in, a glowing light that was like melted silver on the sea. Soon the shore became distinguishable, and the first thing we saw on land was a pair of camels led by their driver; then, on the dock, some Arabs peacefully fishing. Landing took place amid the most deafening uproar imaginable: negroes, negresses, camels, turbans, cudgelings to right and left, and ear-splitting guttural cries. I gulped down a whole bellyful of colours, like a donkey filling himself with hay. Cudgelings play a great role here; everyone who wears clean clothes beats everyone who wears dirty ones, or rather none at all, and when I say clothes I mean a pair of short breeches.

I

You see many gentlemen sauntering along the streets with nothing but a shirt and a long pipe. Except in the very lowest classes, all the women are veiled, and in their noses they wear ornaments that hang down and sway from side to side like the facedrops of a horse. On the other hand, if you don't see their faces, you see their entire bosoms. As you change countries, you find that modesty changes its location, like a bored traveller who keeps shifting from the outside to the inside of the stage-coach. One curious thing here is the respect, or rather the terror, that everyone displays in the presence of 'Franks', as they call Europeans. We have had bands of ten or twelve Arabs, advancing across the whole width of a street, break apart to let us pass. In fact, Alexandria is almost a European city, there are so many Europeans here. At table in our hotel alone there are thirty, and the place is full of Englishmen, Italians, etc. Yesterday we saw a magnificent procession celebrating the circumcision of the son of a rich merchant. This morning we saw Cleopatra's Needles (two great obelisks on the shorefront), Pompey's column, the catacombs, and Cleopatra's baths. Tomorrow we leave for Rosetta, whence we shall return in three or four days. We go slowly and don't get overtired, living sensibly and clad in flannel from head to foot, even though the temperature indoors is sometimes thirty degrees. The heat is not at all unbearable, thanks to the sea breeze.

Soliman Pasha, the most powerful man in Egypt, the terror of Constantinople – he won the battle of Nezib – happens just now to be in Alexandria instead of Cairo. We paid him a visit yesterday, and presented Lauvergne's letter. He received us very graciously. He is to give us orders for all the provincial governors of Egypt and offered us his carriage for the journey to Cairo. It was he who arranged about our horses for tomorrow. He is charming, cordial, etc. He apparently likes the way we look. In addition, we have M. Galis, chief of the army engineers, Princeteau Bey, etc., just to give you an idea of how we are to travel. We have been given soldiers to hold back the crowd when we want to photograph: I trust you are impressed. As you see, poor old darling, conditions couldn't be better . . . Don't worry, I'll come back in good shape. I have put on so much weight since I left that two pairs of my trousers are with M. Chavannes, a French tailor, being let out to accommodate my paunch.

So – goodbye, old lady. I was interrupted during the writing of this letter by the arrival of M. Pastré, the banker who is to send us our money as we need it and will ship home any packages, in case we buy a mummy or two. Now we are going to our friend Soliman Pasha to pick up a letter from him about tomorrow's expedition: it is addressed to the Governor of Rosetta, seeing to it that he puts us up in his house – i.e., in the fort, apparently the only place to stay. We had intended to push on as far as Damietta. But as we have been told that that would be too tiring on horseback because of the sand, we have given up the idea. We'll go to Cairo by boat. As you see, we're not stubborn; it's our principle to follow the advice of experts and to behave like a pair of little saints. Goodbye, a thousand kisses, kiss the baby for me, send me long letters . . .

The Same to the Same

Alexandria, Thursday, 22 [November 1849]
My darling – I am writing you in white tie and tails, pumps, etc., like a man who has been paying a call on a prime minister: in fact we have just left Hartim Bey, Minister of Foreign Affairs, to whom we were introduced by the [French] consul and who received us splendidly. He is going to give us a *firman* with his seal on it for our entire journey. It is unbelievable how well we are treated here – it's as though we were princes, and I'm not joking. Sassetti keeps saying: 'Whatever happens, I'll be

able to say that once in my life I had ten slaves to serve me and one to chase away the flies,' and that is quite true.

. . . Friday morning. [*23 November.*]
We set out at daybreak last Sunday, saddled and booted, harnessed and armed, with four men running behind us, our dragoman on his mule carrying our coats and supplies, and our three horses, which were ridden with simple halters. They looked like nags but were on the contrary excellent beasts; with two pricks of the spur they were off at a gallop, and a whistle brought them up short. To make them go right or left you had only to touch their neck. The desert begins at the very gates of Alexandria: first sandy hillocks covered here and there with palms, and then dunes that stretch on endlessly. From time to time you see on the horizon what looks like great stretches of water with trees reflected in them, and at their farthest limit, where they seem to touch the sky, a grey vapour that appears to be moving in a rush, like a train: that is the mirage, known to all, Arabs and Europeans – people familiar with the desert as well as those seeing it for the first time. Now and then you come upon the carcass of some animal on the sand – a dead camel three-quarters eaten by jackals, its guts exposed and blackened by

the sun; a mummified buffalo, a horse's head, etc. Arabs trot by on their donkeys, their wives bundled in immense black or white veils: you exchange greetings – *'Taïeb'* – and continue on your way. About eleven o'clock we lunched near Abukir, in a fort manned by soldiers who gave us excellent coffee and refused *baksheesh* (a wonder!). The beach at Abukir is in places still littered with the wreckage of ships. We saw a number of sharks that had been washed up, and our horses trod on shells at the edge of the sea. We shot cormorants and water-magpies, and our Arabs ran like hares to pick up those we wounded: I brought down a few birds myself – yes, *me*! – something new, what? The weather was magnificent, sea and sky bluest blue, an immensity of space.

At a place called Edku (you will find it on your map) we took a ferry and there our runners bought some dates from a camel-driver whose two beasts were laden with them. A mile or two farther on, we were riding tranquilly along side by side, a hundred feet in front of our runners, when suddenly we heard loud cries from behind. We turned, and saw our men in a tumult, jostling and pushing one another and making signs for us to turn back. Sassetti dashed off at a gallop, his velvet jacket streaming out behind him; and digging our spurs into our horses we followed after to the scene of the conflict. It was occasioned, we discovered, by the owner of the dates, who had been following his camels at a distance and who, coming upon our men and seeing that they were eating dates, had thought they had stolen them and had fallen on them with his cudgel.

But when he saw us three ruffians descending upon him with rifles slung over our saddles, roles were reversed, and from the beater he became the beaten. Courage returned to our men, and they fell upon him with their sticks in such a way that his backside was soon resounding with blow after blow. To escape, he ran into the sea, lifting up his robe to keep it dry, but his assailants followed. The higher he lifted his robe, the greater the area he exposed to their cudgels, which rattled on him like drumsticks. You can't imagine anything funnier than that man's black behind amidst the white foam churned up by the combat. The rest of us stood on the shore, laughing like fools; my sides still ache when I think of it . . . Two days later, coming back from Rosetta, we met the same camels as they were returning from Alexandria. Perceiving us from afar, the owner hastily left his beasts and made a long detour in the desert to avoid us – a precaution which diverted us considerably. You would scarcely believe the important role played by the cudgel in this part of the world; buffets are distributed with a sublime prodigality, always accompanied by loud cries; it's the most genuine kind of local colour you can think of.

At six in the evening, after a sunset that made the sky look like melted vermilion and the sand of the desert like ink, we arrived at Rosetta and found all the gates closed. At the name of Soliman Pasha they opened, creaking faintly like the doors of a barn. The streets were dark, and so narrow that there was just room for a single horseman. We rode through the bazaars, where each shop was lit by a glass of oil hanging from a cord, and arrived at the barracks. The Pasha received us on his sofa, surrounded by negroes who brought us pipes and coffee. After many courtesies and compliments, we were given supper and shown to our beds, which were equipped with excellent mosquito-netting . . . The next morning while we were washing the Pasha came into our room, followed by the regimental doctor, an Italian who spoke French perfectly and did us the honours of the city. Thanks to him we spent a very agreeable day. When he learned my name and that I was the son of a doctor, he said he had heard of Father and had often seen his name cited. It was no small satisfaction to me, dear Mother, to think that Father's memory was still useful to me, serving as a kind of protection at this distance. That reminds me that in the depths of Brittany, too, at Guérande, the local doctor told me he had quoted Father in his thesis. Yes, poor darling, I think constantly of those who are gone; as my body continues on its journey, my thoughts keep turning back and bury themselves in days past.

. . . All morning was taken up with things to do in Rosetta. By the way, when you write to Rouen will you please make inquiries about M. Julienne, who invented those fuel-saving devices for steam pumps? What is his address? Would he like to enter into correspondence with M. Foucault, manager of rice production at Rosetta, to whom I spoke of this invention and who would like to hear more? . . . I promised to do this, and would like to keep my word . . .

From Flaubert's Travel Notes

Sunday morning, 25 [November 1849] From Alexandria to Cairo. Leave on a boat towed by a small steamer carrying only its engine. Flat, dead banks of the Mahmudiyeh; on the shore a few naked Arabs running; from time to time, a traveller trots by on horseback, swathed in white in his Turkish saddle. Passengers: . . . an English family, hideous; the mother looks like a sick old parrot (because of the green eyeshade attached to her bonnet) . . . At 'Atfeh you enter the Nile and take a larger boat.

First night on the Nile. State of contentment and of lyricism: I gesticulate, recite lines from Bouilhet, cannot bring myself to go to bed; I think of Cleopatra. The water is yellow and very smooth; a few stars. Well wrapped in my pelisse, I fall asleep on my camp-bed, on deck. Such rapture! I awoke before Maxime; in waking, he stretched out his left hand instinctively, to see if I was there.

On one side, the desert; on the other, a green meadow. With its sycamores it resembles from a distance a Norman plain with its apple-trees. The desert is a reddish-grey. Two of the Pyramids come into view, then a smaller one. To our left, Cairo appears, huddled on a hill; the dome of the mosque of Mohammed Ali; behind it, the bare Mokattam hills.

From Flaubert's Travel Notes

Soirée chez la Triestine. Little street behind the Hôtel d'Orient. We are taken upstairs into a large room. The divan projects out over the street; on both sides of the divan, small windows giving on the street, which cannot be shut. Opposite the divan, a large window without frame or glass; through it we see a palm-tree. On a large divan to the left, two women sitting cross-legged; on a kind of mantel-piece, a night-light and a bottle of raki. La Triestina comes down, a small woman, blonde, red-faced. The first of the two women – thick-lipped, snub-nosed, gay, brutal. '*Un poco matta, Signor,*' said La Triestina; the second, large black eyes, straight nose, tired plaintive air, probably the mistress of some European in Cairo. She understands two or three words of French and knows what the Cross of the Legion of Honour is. La Triestina was violently afraid of the police, begged us to make no noise. Abbas Pasha, who is fond only of men, makes things difficult for women; in this brothel it is forbidden to dance or play music. Nevertheless she played the *darabukeh* on the table with her fingers, while the other rolled her girdle, knotted it low on her hips, and danced; she did an Alexandrian dance which consists, as to arm move-ments, in raising the edge of each hand alternately to the forehead. Another dance: arms stretched out front, elbows a little bent, the torso motionless; the pelvis quivers. Preliminary ablutions of *ces dames*. A litter of kittens had to be removed from my bed. Hadely did not undo her jacket, making signs to show me she had a pain in her chest.

Effect: she in front of me, the rustle of her

clothes, the sound made by the gold piastres of her snood – a clear, slow sound. Moonlight. She carried a torch.

On the matting: firm flesh, bronze arse, shaven cunt, dry though fatty; the whole thing gave the effect of a plague victim or a leperhouse. She helped me get back into my clothes. Her words in Arabic that I did not understand. They were questions of three or four words, and she waited for the answer; our eyes entered into each other's; the intensity of our gaze doubled. Joseph's expression amid all this. Love-making by interpreter.

Flaubert to Louis Bouilhet

Cairo, Saturday night, 10 o'clock
1 December 1849

Let me begin by giving you a great hug, holding my breath as long as possible, so that as I exhale on to this paper your spirit will be near me. I imagine that you must be thinking quite a bit about us. For we think quite a bit about you, and miss you a hundred times a day. Yesterday, for example, my dear sir, we were at the cat-house. But let's not jump ahead. At the present moment the moon is shining on the minarets – all is silence but for the occasional barking of dogs. My curtains are pulled back, and outside my window is the mass of the trees in the garden, black against the pale glimmer of the night. I am writing on a table with a green cloth, lit by two candles, and taking my ink from an ointment jar: near me, about ten millimetres away, are my ministerial instructions, which seem to be waiting impatiently for the day I'll use them as toilet paper. Behind the partition I hear the young Maxime, preparing solutions for his negatives. Upstairs sleep the mutes, namely Sassetti and the dragoman, the latter, if truth be known, one of the most arrant pimps, ruffians and old bardashes that could ever be imagined. As for my lordship, I am wearing a large white cotton Nubian shirt, trimmed with little pompoms and of a cut whose description would take up too much space here. My head is completely shaved except for one lock at the occiput (by which Mohammed lifts you up on Judgement Day) and adorned with a tarboosh which is of a screaming red and made me half die of heat the first days I wore it. We look quite the pair of orientals – Max is especially marvellous when he smokes his *narghile* and fingers his beads. Considerations of safety limit our sartorial splurges: in Egypt the European is accorded greater respect than the native, so we won't dress up completely until we reach Syria.

. . . I am sure that as an intelligent man you

don't expect me to send you an account of my trip
. . . In a word, this is how I sum up my feelings so
far: very little impressed by nature here – i.e. landscape, sky, desert (except the mirages); enormously
excited by the cities and the people. Hugo would
say that I was closer to God than to mankind. It
probably comes of my having given more imagin-
ation and thought, before coming here, to things
like horizon, greenery, sand, trees, sun, etc., than
to houses, streets, costumes and faces. The result
is that nature has been a rediscovery and the rest
a discovery. There is one new element which I
hadn't expected to see and which is tremendous
here, and that is the grotesque. All the old comic
business of the cudgeled slave, of the coarse traf-
ficker in women, of the thieving merchant – it's
all very fresh here, very genuine and charming. In
the streets, in the houses, on any and all occasions,
there is a merry proliferation of beatings right and
left. There are guttural intonations that sound like
the cries of wild beasts, and laughter, and flowing
white robes, and ivory teeth flashing between thick
lips, and flat negro noses, and dusty feet, and necklaces, and bracelets! Poor you! The pasha at Rosetta
gave us a dinner at which there were ten negroes
to serve us – they wore silk jackets and some had
silver bracelets; and a little negro boy waved away
the flies with a kind of feather-duster made of

rushes. We ate with our fingers, the food was brought one dish at a time on a silver tray – about thirty different dishes made their appearance in this way. We were on divans in a wooden pavilion, windows open on the water. One of the finest things is the camel – I never tire of watching this strange beast that lurches like a turkey and sways its neck like a swan. Their cry is something that I wear myself out trying to imitate – I hope to bring it back with me – but it's hard to reproduce – a rattle with a kind of tremulous gargling as an accompaniment.

. . . The morning we arrived in Egypt . . . we had scarcely set foot on shore when Max, the old lecher, got excited over a negress who was drawing water at a fountain. He is just as excited by little negro boys. By whom is he *not* excited? Or, rather, by *what*? . . . Tomorrow we are to have a party on the river, with several whores dancing to the sound of *darabukehs* and castanets, their hair spangled with gold piastres. I'll try to make my next letter less disjointed – I've been interrupted twenty times in this one – and send you something worthwhile.

From Flaubert's Travel Notes

Departure. Friday [7 December 1849], set out at noon for the Pyramids.

Maxime is mounted on a white horse that keeps jerking its head, Sassetti on a small white horse, myself on a bay, Joseph on a donkey.

We pass Soliman Pasha's gardens. Island of Roda. We cross the Nile in a small boat: while our horses are being led aboard, a corpse in its coffin is borne past us. Energy of our oarsmen: they sing, shouting out the rhythm as they bend forward and back. The sail swells full and we skim along fast.

Gizeh. Mud houses as at 'Atfeh – palm grove. Two waterwheels, one turned by an ox and the other by a camel.

Now stretching out before us is an immense plain, very green, with squares of black soil which are the fields most recently ploughed, the last from which the flood withdrew: they stand out like India ink on the solid green. I think of the invocation to Isis: 'Hail, hail, black soil of Egypt!' The soil of Egypt *is* black. Some buffaloes are grazing, now and again a waterless muddy creek, in which our horses sink to their knees; soon we are crossing great puddles or creeks.

About half-past three we are almost on the edge of the desert, the three Pyramids looming up ahead of us. I can contain myself no longer, and dig in my spurs; my horse bursts into a gallop, splashing through the swamp. Two minutes later Maxime follows suit. Furious race. I begin to shout in spite of myself; we climb rapidly up to the Sphinx, clouds of sand swirling about us. At first our Arabs followed us, crying 'Sphinx! Sphinx! Oh! Oh! Oh!' It grew larger and larger, and rose out of the ground like a dog lifting itself up.

View of the Sphinx. Abu-el-Houl (Father of Terror). The sand, the Pyramids, the Sphinx, all grey and bathed in a great rosy light; the sky perfectly blue, eagles slowly wheeling and gliding around the tips of the Pyramids. We stop before the Sphinx; it fixes us with a terrifying stare; Maxime is quite pale; I am afraid of becoming giddy, and try to control my emotion. We ride off madly at full speed among the stones. We walk around the Pyramids, right at their feet. Our baggage is late in arriving; night falls.

Ascent. Up at five – the first – and wash in front of the tent in the canvas pail. We hear several jackals barking. Ascent of the Great Pyramid, the one to the right (Kheops). The stones, which at a distance of two hundred paces seem the size of paving-blocks, are in reality – the smallest of them – three feet high; generally they come up to our chests. We go up at the left hand corner (opposite the Pyramid of Khephren); the Arabs push and pull me; I am quickly exhausted, it is desperately tiring. I stop five or six times on the way up. Maxime started before me and goes fast. Finally I reach the top.

We wait a good half hour for the sunrise.

The sun was rising just opposite; the whole valley of the Nile, bathed in mist, seemed to be a still white sea; and the desert behind us, with its hillocks of sand, another ocean, deep purple, its waves all petrified. But as the sun climbed behind the Arabian chain the mist was torn into great shreds of filmy gauze; the meadows, cut by canals, were like green lawns with winding borders. To sum up: three colours – immense green at my feet in the foreground; the sky pale red – worn vermilion; behind and to the right, a rolling expanse looking scorched and iridescent, with the minarets of Cairo, *canges* passing in the distance, clusters of palms.

Finally the sky shows a streak of orange where the sun is about to rise. Everything between the horizon and us is all white and looks like an ocean; this recedes and lifts. The sun, it seems, is moving fast and climbing above oblong clouds that look like swan's down, of an inexpressible softness; the trees in the groves around the villages (Gizeh, Matariyeh, Bedrashein, etc.) seem to be in the sky itself, for the entire perspective is perpendicular, as I once saw it before, from the Port de la Picade in the Pyrenees; behind us, when we turn around, is the desert – purple waves of sand, a purple ocean.

The light increases. There are two things: the dry desert behind us, and before us an immense, delightful expanse of green, furrowed by endless canals, dotted here and there with tufts of palms; then, in the background, a little to the left, the minarets of Cairo and especially the mosque of Mohammed Ali (imitating Santa Sophia), towering above the others. (On the side of the Pyramid lit by the rising sun I see a business card: '*Humbert, Frotteur*' fastened to the stone. Pathetic condition of Maxime, who had raced up ahead of me to put it there; he nearly died of breathlessness.) Easy descent down the opposite face.

Interior of the Great Pyramid. After breakfast we visit the interior of the Pyramid. The opening is on the north. Smooth, even corridor (like a sewer), which you descend; then another corridor ascends; we slip on bat's dung. It seems that these corridors were made to allow the huge coffins to be drawn slowly into place. Before the king's chamber, wider corridors with great longitudinal grooves in the stone, as though a portcullis or something of the kind had been lowered there. King's chamber, all of granite in enormous blocks, empty sarcophagus at the far end. Queen's chamber, smaller, same square shape, probably communicating with the king's chamber.

As we emerge on hands and knees from one of the corridors, we meet a party of Englishmen who are coming in; they are in the same position as we; exchange of civilities; each party proceeds on its way.

Sphinx. We sit on the sand smoking our pipes and staring at it. Its eyes still seem full of life; the left side is stained white by bird-droppings (the tip of the Pyramid of Khephren has the same long white stains); it exactly faces the rising sun, its head is grey, ears very large and protruding like a negro's, its neck is eroded; from the front it is seen in its entirety thanks to a great hollow dug in the sand; the fact that the nose is missing increases the flat, negroid effect. Besides, it was certainly Ethiopian; the lips are thick.

After we looked at the second Pyramid, our

three Englishmen came to pay us a visit in our tent (we had invited them); coffee, *chibouks* [long pipes], fantasia staged by our Arab riders. Wriggling of the old sheik, his hands clasped on his stick. The Arabs crouch and jump up, clapping their hands and singing a Bedouin song meaning 'Round and round and round.'

. . . At night, strong wind; struck by great gusts, the tent shudders and flaps like the sail of a ship.

Sunday. A cold morning, spent photographing; I pose on tip of a pyramid – the one at the S.E. corner of the Great Pyramid.

In the afternoon we ride in the desert . . . We pass between the first and second Pyramids and soon come to a valley of sand, seemingly scooped out by a single great gust of wind. Great expanses of stone that look like lava. We gallop for a while, blowing our horns to try them; silence. We have the impression that we are on a beach and are about to see the sea; our moustaches taste of salt, the wind is sharp and bracing, footprints of jack-als and camels half obliterated by the wind. One keeps expecting to see something new from the top of each hill, and each time it's only the desert.

We ride back; the sun is setting. Beyond, the green Egypt; to the left, a slope that is entirely white, one would swear it was snow; the foreground is all purple – the small stones covering the ground glitter, literally bathed in purple light; it is as though one were looking at them through water so transparent as to be invisible; coated with this light as though with enamel, the gravel gleams with a metallic sheen. A jackal runs up and disappears to the right: at this hour of nightfall one hears them barking. Back to the tent, skirting the base of the Pyramid of Khephren, which seems to me inordinately huge and completely sheer; it's like a cliff, like a thing of nature, a mountain – as though it had been created just as it is, and with something terrible about it, as if it were going to crush you. It is at sunset that the Pyramids must be seen.

Tuesday morning, 11 [December]. Walk along the shore of the pond with our rifles over our shoulders . . . Pipe and coffee; we shoot some turtledoves that are standing around the hole in which lies a colossus (Sesostris?) flat on its face in the water; some of the birds are perched on the statue itself.

We mount our horses and ride across cultivated fields and down a long dusty path toward the pyramids of Sakkara. . . . Enormous number of scorpions. Arabs come up and offer us yellowed skulls and painted wooden panels. The soil seems to be composed of human debris; to adjust my horse's bridle my *saïs* took up a fragment of bone. The ground is pitted and mounded from diggings; everything is up and down; it would be dangerous to gallop over this treacherous plain. Camels pass, a black boy leading them.

To get some ibises we go down into a hole and then crawl along a passageway almost on our stomachs, inching over fine sand and fragments of pottery; at the far end the jars containing ibises are stacked like blocks of sugar at a grocer's, head to foot.

Rock tomb. [Mastaba of Ti.] Underground burial chamber. A narrow opening leads down through the sand: square, half-buried columns, remains of paintings and a very beautiful drawing: chambers vaulted with convex longitudinal stone blocks; modillions supporting the cornices, niches for mummies. It must have been a very beautiful place.

Return from Abusir to Memphis at a gallop.

We read our notes on Memphis, lying on the rug; fleas jump on the pages. Walk at sunset in the palm groves: their shadow stretches over the green of the crops, as columns must once have cast their shadows over now vanished pavements. The palm – an architectural tree. Everything in Egypt seems made for architecture – the planes of the fields, the vegetation, the human anatomy, the horizon lines.

Wednesday. Return to Cairo, riding under palms almost all the way. The dust around their feet is dappled with filtered sunlight; a field of flowering beans gives off fragrance; the sun is hot and good. I see a scarab under the feet of my horse. We cross the Nile at Bedrashein, leaving Tura, on the other bank, a bit to the right.

Large expanse of sand as far as the Tombs of the Mamelukes – good sun, the feeling of being on the road; dust, heat. I grip my horse with my knees and sit slouching, head down. We enter the city past the prison and the citadel.

Wednesday the 12th was my birthday – twenty-eight.

Flaubert to his Mother

Cairo, 5 January 1850

. . . I'm bursting to tell you my name. Do you know what the Arabs call me? Since they have great difficulty in pronouncing French names, they invent their own for us Franks. Can you guess? Abu-Chanab, which means 'Father of the Moustache'. That word, *abu*, father, is applied to everything connected with the chief detail that is being spoken about – thus for merchants selling various commodities they say Father of the Shoes,

Father of the Glue, Father of the Mustard, etc. Max's name is a very long one which I don't remember, and which means 'the man who is excessively thin'. Imagine my joy when I learned the honour being paid to that particular part of myself.

. . . Often when we have been out since early morning and feel hungry and don't want to take time to return to the hotel for lunch, we sit down in a Turkish restaurant. Here all the carving is done with one's hands, and everyone belches to his heart's content. Dining-room and kitchen are all one, and behind you at the great fireplace little pots bubble and steam under the eye of the chef in his white turban and rolled-up sleeves. I am careful to write down the names of all the dishes and their ingredients. Also, I have made a list of all the perfumes that are made in Cairo; it may be very useful to me somewhere. We have hired two dragomans. In the evening an Arab story-teller comes and reads us stories, and there is an effendi whom we pay to make translations for us.

. . . A few days ago I spent a fine afternoon. Max stayed at home to do I forget what, and I took Hasan (the second dragoman we have temporarily hired) and paid a visit to the bishop of the Copts for the sake of a conversation with him. I entered a square courtyard surrounded by columns, with a little garden in the middle – that is, a few big trees and a bed of dark greenery, around which ran a trellised wooden divan. My dragoman, with his wide trousers and his large-sleeved jacket, walked ahead; I behind. On one of the corners of the divan was sitting a scowling old personage with a long white beard, wearing an ample pelisse; books in a baroque kind of handwriting were strewn all about him. At a certain distance were standing three black-robed theologians, younger and also with long beards. The dragoman said: 'This is a French gentleman (*cawadja fransaoui*) who is travelling all over the world in search of knowledge, and who has come to you to speak of your religion.' Such is the kind of language they go in for here. Can you imagine how I talk to them? A while ago when I was looking at seeds in a shop a woman to whom I had given something said: 'Blessings on you, my sweet lord: God grant that you return safe and sound to your native land.' There is much use of such blessings and ritual formulas. When Max asked a groom if he wasn't tired, the answer was: 'The pleasure of being seen by you suffices.'

But to return to the bishop. He received me with many courtesies; coffee was brought, and soon I began to ask questions concerning the Trinity, the Virgin, the Gospels, the Eucharist – all my old erudition of *Saint Anthony* came back in a flood. It was superb, the sky blue above us, the trees, the books spread out, the old fellow ruminating in his beard before answering me, myself sitting cross-legged beside him, gesticulating with my pencil and taking notes, while Hasan stood motionless, translating aloud, and the three other theologians, sitting on stools, nodded their heads and inter-jected an occasional few words. I enjoyed it deeply. That was indeed the old Orient, land of religions and flowing robes. When the bishop gave out, one of the theologians replaced him; and when I finally saw that they were all somewhat flushed, I left. I am going back, for there is much to learn in that place. The Coptic religion is the most ancient of existing Christian sects, and little or nothing is known about it in Europe (so far as I know). I am going to talk with the Armenians, too, and the Greeks, and the Sunnites, and especially with Moslem scholars.

We are still waiting for the return of the cara-van from Mecca; it is too good an event to miss, and we shall not leave for Upper Egypt until the pilgrims have arrived. There are some bizarre things to see, we have been told: priests' horses walking over prostrate bodies of the faithful, all kinds of dervishes, singers, etc.

. . . When I think of my future (that happens

rarely, for I generally think of nothing at all despite the elevated thoughts one should have in the presence of ruins!), when I ask myself: 'What shall I do when I return? What path shall I follow?' and the like, I am full of doubts and indecision. At every stage in my life I have shirked facing my problems in just this same way; and I shall die at eighty before having formed any opinion concerning myself or, perhaps, without writing anything that would have shown me what I could do. Is *Saint Anthony* good or bad? That is what I often ask myself, for example: who was mistaken, I or the others? However, I worry very little about any of this; I live like a plant, filling myself with sun and light, with colours and fresh air. I keep eating, so to speak; afterwards the digesting will have to be done, then the shitting; and the shit had better be good! That's the important thing.

. . . You ask me whether the Orient is up to what I imagined it to be. Yes, it is; and more than that, it extends far beyond the narrow idea I had of it. I have found, clearly delineated, everything that was hazy in my mind. Facts have taken the place of suppositions – so excellently so that it is often as though I were suddenly coming upon old forgotten dreams.

Flaubert to Louis Bouilhet

Cairo, 15 January 1850

. . . I'm greatly giving myself over to the study of perfumes and to the composition of ointments. Yesterday I ate half a pastille so heating that for three hours I thought my tongue was on fire. I haunt the Turkish baths. I devoured the lines from *Melaenis*. Come, let's be calm: no one incapable of restraint was ever a writer – at this moment I'm bursting – I'd like to let off steam and use you as a punching-bag – everything's mixed up and jostling everything else in my sick brain – let's try for some order. . . .

De Saltatoribus

We have not yet seen any dancing girls; they are all in exile in Upper Egypt. Good brothels no longer exist in Cairo, either. The party we were to have had on the Nile the last time I wrote you fell through – no loss there. But we have seen male dancers. Oh! Oh! Oh!

That was us, calling you. I was indignant and very sad that you were not here. Three or four musicians playing curious instruments (we'll bring some home) took up their positions at the end of the hotel dining room while one gentleman was still eating his lunch and the rest of us were sitting on the divan smoking our pipes. As dancers, imagine two rascals, quite ugly, but charming in their corruption, in their obscene leerings and the femininity of their movements, dressed as women, their eyes painted with antimony. For costume, they had wide trousers . . . From time to time, during the dance, the impresario, or pimp, who brought them plays around them, kissing them on the belly, the arse, and the small of the back, and making obscene remarks in an effort to put additional spice into a thing that is already quite clear in itself. It is too beautiful to be exciting. I doubt whether we shall find the women as good as the men; the ugliness of the latter adds greatly to the thing as art. I had a headache for the rest of the day, and I had to go and pee two or three times during the performance – a nervous reaction that I attribute particularly to the music. – I'll have this marvellous Hasan el-Belbeissi come again. He'll dance the Bee for me, in particular. Done by such a bardash as he, it can scarcely be a thing for babes.

Speaking of bardashes, this is what I know about them. Here it is quite accepted. One admits one's sodomy, and it is spoken of at table in the hotel. Sometimes you do a bit of denying, and then every-

body teases you and you end up confessing.
Travelling as we are for educational purposes, and
charged with a mission by the government, we have
considered it our duty to indulge in this form of ejac-
ulation. So far the occasion has not presented itself.
We continue to seek it, however. It's at the baths that
such things take place. You reserve the bath for yourself (five francs including masseurs, pipe, coffee,
sheet and towel) and you skewer your lad in one of
the rooms. Be informed, furthermore, that all the
bath-boys are bardashes. The final masseurs, the ones
who come to rub you when all the rest is done, are
usually quite nice young boys. We had our eye on
one in an establishment very near our hotel. I
reserved the bath exclusively for myself. I went, and
the rascal was away that day! I was alone in the hot
room, watching the daylight fade through the great
circles of glass in the dome. Hot water was flowing
everywhere; stretched out indolently I thought of a
quantity of things as my pores tranquilly dilated. It
is very voluptuous and sweetly melancholy to take
a bath like that quite alone, lost in those dim rooms
where the slightest noise resounds like a cannon shot,
while the naked *kellaas* call out to one another as
they massage you, turning you over like embalmers
preparing you for the tomb. That day (the day before
yesterday, Monday) my *kellaa* was rubbing me gently,
and when he came to the noble parts he lifted up

my *boules d'amour* to clean them, then continuing to rub my chest with his left hand he began to pull with his right on my prick, and as he drew it up and down he leaned over my shoulder and said '*baksheesh, baksheesh.*' He was a man in his fifties, ignoble, disgusting – imagine the effect, and the word '*baksheesh, baksheesh.*' I pushed him away a little, saying '*làh, làh*' ('no, no') – he thought I was angry and took on a craven look – then I gave him a few pats on the shoulder, saying '*làh, làh*' again but more gently – he smiled a smile that meant, 'You're not fooling me – you like it as much as anybody, but today you've decided against it for some reason.' As for me, I laughed aloud like a dirty old man, and the shadowy vault of the bath echoed with the sound.

Flaubert to his Mother

Cairo, 3 February 1850

. . . I saw dervishes who had iron spikes passed through their mouths and their chests, with oranges stuck on both ends of the spike. The crowd of the faithful was shouting with enthusiasm. Add to that, music wild enough to drive one crazy. When the sheik (the priest) on horseback appeared, the jolly crew lay down on the ground, heads to feet. They arranged themselves in a row like herrings, each one pressed close to the next so that there was not the slightest space between their bodies. A man walked over them, to make sure that this human plank would hold; and then, to drive back the crowd, a hail, a tempest, a hurricane, a veritable tornado of bastinados was rained right and left by the eunuchs on anyone who happened to be within reach. (We were up on a wall, Sassetti and Joseph just below us. We stayed there from eleven until nearly four. It was very cold, and there was scarcely room for us to move, the crowd was so dense and our perch so narrow. But it was excellent and we missed nothing.) We heard the thud of palmwood truncheons on tarbooshes, as though someone were clubbing bales of oakum or wool. That is exactly how it sounded. The sheik then advanced, his horse led by two grooms and he himself supported in the saddle by two others. The poor fellow needed them – his hands were beginning to shake, and he was clearly having an attack of nerves: by the end of his ride he was almost fainting. His horse walked slowly over the bodies of the more than two hundred men lying flat on the ground. It was impossible to learn anything about those who died as a result: the crowd pushed so close behind the sheik as he advanced that one could no more ascertain the fate of those poor wretches than learn what happens to a pin thrown into a river.

Just the evening before, we had been in a monastery of dervishes where we saw one fall into convulsions from shouting 'Allah!' These are very fine sights, which would have brought many a good laugh from M. de Voltaire. Imagine his remarks about the poor old human mind! About fanaticism! Superstition! None of it made me laugh in the slightest, and it is all too *absorbing* to be appalling. The most terrible thing is their music.

This is indeed a funny country. Yesterday, for example, we were at a café which is one of the best in Cairo, and where there were, at the same time as ourselves, inside, a donkey shitting and a gentleman who was pissing in a corner. No one finds that odd; no one says anything. Sometimes a man beside you will get up and begin to say his prayers, with great bowings and exclaimings, as though he were quite alone. No one even turns his head to look, it is all so natural. Can you imagine someone suddenly saying grace in the Café de Paris?

From Flaubert's Travel Notes

6 February 1850 . . . Today I am on the Nile and we have just passed Memphis.

We left Old Cairo with a good north wind. Our two sails, their angles intersecting, swelled to their entire width, and the *cange* skimmed along, heeling, its keel cutting the water. Sitting cross-legged in the bow, our Raïs Ibrahim stared ahead, and from time to time, without turning around, called back an order to the crew. Standing on the poop that forms the roof of our cabin, the mate held the tiller, smoking his black wooden *chibouk*. The sun was bright, the sky blue. With our glass we saw herons and storks here and there on the banks.

The water of the Nile is quite yellow; it carries a good deal of soil. One might think of it as being weary of all the countries it has crossed, weary of endlessly murmuring the same monotonous complaint that it has traveled too far. If the Niger and the Nile are but one and the same river, where does this water come from? What has it seen? Like the ocean, this river sends our thoughts back almost incalculable distances; then there is the eternal dream of Cleopatra, and the great memory of the sun, the golden sun of the Pharaohs. As evening fell, the sky turned all red to the right, all pink to the left. The pyramids of Sakkara stood out sharp and grey against the vermilion backdrop of the horizon. An incandescence glowed in all that part of the sky, drenching it with a golden light. On the other bank, to the left, everything was pink; the closer to the earth, the deeper the pink. The pink lifted and paled, becoming yellow, then greenish; then the green itself paled, and almost imperceptibly, through white, became the blue which made the vault above our heads, where there was the final melting of the transition (abrupt) between the two great colours.

Dance of the sailors. Joseph at his stoves. The boat heeling. The Nile in the middle of the landscape; and we in the middle of the Nile. Tufts of palm-trees grow at the base of the pyramids of Sakkara like nettles at the foot of graves.

From Flaubert's Travel Notes

Monday, [11 *February* 1850] . . . Golden clouds, like satin sofas. The sky is full of bluish, pigeon's-breast tints: the sun is setting in the desert. To the left, the Arabian chain with its indentations; it is flat on top, a plateau, in the foreground, palms, and this foreground is bathed in darkness; in the middle ground, beyond the palms, camels pass, and two or three Arabs riding donkeys. What silence! Not a sound. Two great strips of sand, and the sun! One sees how awesome it might be here. The Sphinx has something of the same effect.

Kena. Sunday morning, [3 March 1850] . . . The bazaars smell of coffee and sandalwood. At the bend of one of the streets, to the right as you leave the bazaar, we suddenly find ourselves in the quarter of the *almehs* [prostitutes]. The street curves a little; the houses, of grey earth, are no more than four feet high. To the left, sloping down toward the Nile, another street and a palm-tree. Blue sky. The women are sitting in their doorways on mats, or standing. Light-coloured robes, one over the other, hang loosely in the hot wind; blue robes around the bodies of the negresses. The clothes are sky-blue, bright yellow, pink, red – all contrasting with the differently coloured skins. Necklaces of gold piastres falling to their knees; on their heads, piastres threaded on silk and attached to the ends of the hair – they tinkle. The negresses have vertical knife-marks on their cheeks, usually three on each cheek: this is done in infancy, with a red-hot knife.

Fat woman (Mme Maurice) in blue, deep-set dark eyes, square chin, small hands, eyebrows heavily painted, pleasant-looking. Girl with frizzy hair brought down over her forehead, slightly marked by smallpox (in the street that continues the bazaar, going straight ahead to Bir 'Ambar, past the Greek grocery). Another was wearing a striped Syrian *habar* [hooded robe]. Tall girl with such a soft voice, calling *'Cawadja! Cawadja!'* The sun was very strong.

. . . We return to the street of the *almehs*. I walk along it deliberately: they call out to me: 'Cawadja, cawadja, baksheesh! Baksheesh! Cawadja!' I give some of them a few piastres; a few put their arms around me and try to pull me inside: I deliberately abstain from going with them, lest it spoil the sweet sadness of it all, and I walk away.

. . . At night a few stars are reflected in the water, elongated there like the flames of great torches. During the day, in the sun, a diamond star glitters at the tip of each wave.

Monday, 4 March . . . Sunset over Medinet Habu. The mountains are dark indigo (on the Medinet Habu side); blue over dark grey, with contrasting horizontal stripes of purplish red in the clefts of the valleys. The palms are black as ink, the sky is red, the Nile has the look of a lake of molten steel.

When we arrived off Thebes our sailors were drumming on their *darabukehs*, the mate was playing his flute, Khalil was dancing with his castanets: they broke off to land.

It was then, as I was enjoying those things, and just as I was watching three wave-crests bending under the wind behind us, that I felt a surge of solemn happiness that reached out towards what I was seeing, and I thanked God in my heart for having made me capable of such a joy: I felt fortunate at the thought, and yet it seemed to me that I was thinking of nothing: it was a sensuous pleasure that pervaded my entire being.

Saturday, 9 March 1850. Assuan. Reached Assuan threading our course between the rocks in midstream; they are dark chocolate-colour, with long white streaks of bird-droppings that widen towards the bottom. To the right, bare sand-hills, their summits sharp against the blue sky. The light comes down perpendicular into transparent depths. A negro landscape . . .

In a shop we see an *almeh*, tall, slender, black – or rather, green – frizzy negro hair. Her eyes are dreamy and sad, or, rather, suggestive of negro daydreaming. She rolls her eyes – she is charming in profile. Another, little woman with tousled frizzy hair under her tarboosh – this one is cheerful.

Azizeh. The tall girl is named Azizeh. Her dancing is more expert than Kuchuk's. For dancing she takes off her flowing robe and puts on a cotton dress of European cut. She begins. Her neck slides back and forth on her vertebrae, and more often sideways, as though her head were going to fall off; terrifying effect of decapitation.

She stands on one foot, lifts the other, the knee making a right angle, then brings it down firmly.

This is no longer Egypt; it is negro, African, savage – as wild as the other was formal.

Another dance: putting the left foot in the place of the right, and the right in the place of the left, alternately and very fast.

The blanket that served as rug in her hut became wrinkled; she stopped from time to time to pull it straight.

She stripped. On her belly she wore a belt of coloured beads. Her long necklace of gold piastres descended to her vagina, and she passed the end of it through the bead belt.

Furious jerking of the hips. The face always expressionless. A little girl of two or three, affected by the music, tried to imitate her, and danced herself, making no sound.

This was in an earthen hut, scarcely high enough for a woman to stand erect, in a section outside the city that was almost completely reduced to ruins. In the midst of this silence, these women in red and gold.

On the shore, a man holding ostrich plumes offers them to us for sale.

Good Friday. Clearing: '*aou-afi, aou-afi.*'* Arched body of a frizzy-haired little negro, ugly, his eyes

* Colloquial greeting among fellahin

sore from the dust, who was carrying a jar of milk on his head.

In the small temple, many wasps' nests, especially in the corners.

Reflection: the Egyptian temples bore me profoundly. Are they going to become like the churches in Brittany, the waterfalls in the Pyrenees? Oh necessity! To do what you are supposed to do; to be always, according to the circumstances (and despite the aversion of the moment), what a young man, or a tourist, or an artist, or a son, or a citizen, etc. is supposed to be!

31 March [1850]. *Easter Sunday*. In the afternoon, reach ancient Ibrim, on the right bank of the Nile. While Max took a picture of the fort from below, I slowly climbed the side of the hill, breaking my toenails on rough stones that had rolled down from above. The soil is like cinders. Three or four Arabs passed me on the right, riding donkeys. I walk around the citadel, looking for a way in; finally I find one on the plateau, facing east.

The interior is an entire city enclosed within walls; houses all in ruins and crammed close together or even touching; streets wind between; in the centre, a large square. If you climb on to a wall, the foundations of all those ruined houses – the mere four walls – give a checkerboard effect. Ruins of a mosque, with a granite column bearing a Greek cross; similar columns have been made to serve as door-sills in several places. The entrance gate was on the north side. Through openings in the wall one can see long stretches of the Nile – there are broad islands of sand. On the other side of the Nile, the desert; in the desert middle-ground, a single tree on the right; further off, two on the left.

The whole ruin gives off an effluvium of fever, and makes you think of bored people dying of marasmus; it is the Orient of the Middle Ages, the Mamelukes, the Barbarians. The citadel, built on the crest of the rock, formerly belonged to the Mamelukes, who thus controlled the river. Most of it is built of rough stones – in a very few places, chiefly at the corners, the stones are shaped and fitted.

There is a great silence here – not a soul – I am alone, two birds of prey glide overhead; from the other side of the Nile, in the desert, I hear a man's voice calling someone.

I returned [to the *cange*] as night was slowly falling, and watched the darkness engulf everything. To my left, a long ravine leading to the desert; along the side of the ravine winds a path – a hyena track. There are many around here; in the evening the *raïs* warns us not to wander too far from the boat; last year a Turk and his horse were eaten near the First

Cataract. Maxime, worried because I was away so long, had sent some of the sailors to find me.

Monday, 1 April. Second visit to the fort, with Maxime. The caves of Ibrim, on the riverbank, eight or nine feet above the waterline, are a good joke: they contain absolutely nothing, a discovery that kept me cheerful the entire rest of the day.

We spend the afternoon stretched out on the bow of the boat, on Raïs Ibrahim's mat, talking – and not without a certain sadness and bitterness – about that old topic: literature – sweet and never-ending obsession!

Tuesday, 2 April. Korosko. Khamsin weather – heavy, the sun hidden by clouds. On our arrival here at noon, the heat was like blasts from an oven (literally); one feels one's very lungs (I mean it) seared by the gusts of hot wind . . .

[*10 April.*] *Wednesday morning. Debot.* Temple . . .

Before we cast off, a flat-nosed negro sorcerer comes to tell our fortunes. In a shallow basket full of sand he draws circles, and then draws lines out from each circle. He predicts that I 'will receive two letters at Assuan, that there is an old lady who thinks about me constantly, that I had intended to bring my wife along on the trip but finally decided to come alone; that I want both to travel and to be at home, that in my country there is a very powerful man who is most kindly disposed towards me, and that on my return to my country I'll be showered with honours.'

[*10 April 1850.*] We arrive at Philae about 5 p.m. I take Joseph to Assuan at once, via the desert. We are armed to the teeth, for fear of hyenas; our donkeys keep up a good trot; a young boy of about twelve, charming in his grace and nimbleness and clad in a long white shirt, runs ahead of us carrying a lantern. The blue of the sky is dotted with stars – they are almost like fires – the sky is aflame – a real oriental night. An Arab, riding a camel and singing, came into view from the right, cut across our path and disappeared ahead of us.

At Assuan there is an enormous packet, but nothing for me; Augier's *Gabrielle* is the only thing with my name on it. Plenty of letters for Max and Sassetti: I took that very hard.

Flaubert to his Mother

[*26 April 1850*] [*Mailing date.*] [*Esna*].
We are in full summer. At six in the morning it is normally 20° Réaumur in the shade, and during

the day about 30°. The harvest is long since in, and yesterday we ate a watermelon.

. . . We ourselves are leading a splendid existence. The trip to Nubia is over, and our entire stay in Egypt is approaching its end. Now we are going down, by oar, this great river up which we were borne by our two white sails. We stop at all the ruins. We tie up the boat and go ashore. There is always some temple buried to its shoulders in the sand, partially visible, like an old dug-up skeleton. Gods with heads of ibises and crocodiles are painted on walls white with the droppings of the birds of prey that nest between the stones. We walk among the columns; with our palmwood sticks and our day-dreams, we stir up this old dust; through holes in the temple walls we see the incredibly blue sky and the full Nile winding in the middle of the desert with a fringe of green on each bank. *This is the essence of Egypt.* Often there is a flock of black sheep grazing around us, and some naked little boy, agile as a monkey, with the eyes of a cat, ivory teeth, a silver ring in his right ear, and scars on his face – tattooing done with a red-hot knife. Other times there are poor Arab women covered with rags and necklaces, come to sell Joseph chickens, or gathering goat-dung by hand to feed their meagre fields. One marvellous thing is the light, which makes everything glitter. We are always dazzled in the towns – it is like the butterfly colours of an immense costume ball; the white, yellow or blue clothes stand out in the transparent air – blatant tones that would make any painter faint away.

As for me, I think about what I have always thought about – literature; I try to take hold of everything I see; I'd like to imagine something. But what, I don't know. It seems to me that I have become utterly stupid. In the temples we read travellers' names; they strike us as petty and futile. We never write ours; there are some that must have taken three days to carve, so deeply are they cut in the stone. There are some that you keep meeting everywhere – sublime persistence of stupidity.

From Flaubert's Travel Notes

Saturday, 18 May . . . It is hot; on the right a *khamsin* dust-cloud is moving our way from the direction of the Nile (of which all that we can faintly see now is a few of the palms that line the bank). The dust-cloud grows and comes straight at us – it is like an immense vertical cloud that before enveloping us is already high above us for some time, while its base, to the right, is still distant. It is reddish brown and pale red; now we are in the midst of it. A caravan passes us coming the other way; the men, swathed in *kufiyehs* [headcloths] (the women are thickly veiled) lean forward on the necks of their dromedaries; they pass very close to us, no one speaks; it is like a meeting of ghosts amid clouds. I feel something like terror and furious admiration creep along my spine; I laugh nervously; I must have been very pale, and my enjoyment of the moment was intense. As the caravan passed, it seemed to me that the camels were not touching the ground, that they were breasting ahead with a ship-like movement, that inside the dust-cloud they were raised high above the ground, as though they were wading belly-deep in clouds.

From time to time we meet other caravans. One first sees them as a long horizontal line on the horizon, barely distinguishable from the horizon itself; then that dark line rises above the other, and on it one begins to make out small dots; the small dots themselves rise up – they are the heads of camels walking abreast, swaying regularly along the entire line. Seen foreshortened, they look like the heads of ostriches.

The hot wind comes from the south; the sun looks like a tarnished silver plate; a second dust-spout comes on us. This one advances like the smoke from a conflagration, suet-coloured, with

jet-black tones at the base: it comes . . . and comes
. . . and the curtain is on us, bulging out in volutes
below, with deep black fringes. We are enveloped
by it: the force of the wind is such that we have
to clutch our saddles to stay on. When the worst
of the storm has passed, there comes a hail of small
pebbles carried by the wind: the camels turn their
tails to it, stop, and lie down. We resume our way.

Towards 7.30 in the evening the dromedaries
abruptly change their course and head south. A
few moments later we spy in the darkness a few
low-lying hovels with dromedaries sleeping around
them; it is the village of Lakeita. There is a well
here, good for camels. Ten or so shapeless huts
built of piled-up dry stones and straw mats, inhab-
ited by 'Ababdehs. A few goats are hunting for a
bit of grass between the stones, pigeons are peck-
ing at the remains of the camels' straw, vultures
strut around the huts. No one will sell us milk. A
negress's teat – it hangs down well below her
umbilicus, and so flat that it is scarcely the thick-
ness of the two layers of skin; were she to go on
all fours, it would certainly trail on the ground.

We sleep on our blankets on the ground. At
three I awake; we leave at five, going on foot for
the first hour.

In the middle of the day we stop for four hours
at Gamseh Shems, in a small cave formed by a

fallen rock; I lie down there on my back. When I raise my hand (stretching as I wake) the heat of the wind on it is like the breath of an oven; we have to wrap our handkerchiefs around the pommels of our saddles. Towards four o'clock, on the right, in the black rock, hieroglyphs overlaid with Greek inscriptions: sacrifice to Ammon the Begetter and to Horus. The space between the hills gradually narrows; we are walking in a wide corridor. In the evening, beautiful moon: the shadows of our camels' collars sway on the sand . . .

Tuesday, 21 [May] The trail bends to the left; we descend. The chalky mountains surrounding this plain recall the Mokattam. The sky is full of clouds, the air humid, one feels the sea, our clothes are moist. I long to be there; it is always the same whenever I am nearing a goal: I have patience in all things – as far as the antechamber. A few drops of rain. An hour after leaving the well we come to a place full of reeds and high grass; dromedaries and donkeys are in the midst of it, eating and enjoying themselves. Water flows at the roots of the grass in numerous small streams, which deposit considerable quantities of salt on the ground; this is Wadi Ambagi (Place Where There is Water). The hills subside, we turn to the right. A flat face of reddish rock, to the left, at the entrance to the broader valley which leads, first over stones, then over sand, to Koseir. In my impatience I go on foot, running over the gravel and climbing hillocks, hoping to see the sea a minute sooner. How often in the past I have eaten my heart out with impatience, as pointlessly as now! Finally I see the dark line of the Red Sea against the grey horizon. The Red Sea!

I re-mount my camel, and we proceed over the sand to Koseir. It is as though wind had blown the sea-sand back into this broad valley: it is like the abandoned bed of a gulf. From a distance we see the forward masts of ships . . . Birds of prey are flying about and perched on low sand-dunes. Sea and ships to the right; Koseir ahead, with its white houses. To the right, before turning, a few palms enclosed within white walls: a garden! What a blessing for the eyes!

Wednesday, 22 [*May*]. Stroll in the town. The cafés are big *khans*, or rather *okkels*; they are empty during the day, then they gleam with the lighted *sheeshehs* of the pilgrims to Mecca. We visit the boat the pilgrims are to take . . . These Red Sea boats are terrifying: they reek of the plague; to step on board is frightening; thank God I don't have to sail in one. For latrines, there is a kind of wooden balcony, or armchair, fastened outside the gunwale:

if the sea were a bit rough one would inevitably be washed away. The divan and cabin are in the poop – they have no flooring and are filled with freight. Men playing cards with little leather disks printed in colour – there were suns, swords, etc. In the evening, at sunset, we swim. What a swim! How deliciously I lolled in the water!

Flaubert to Louis Bouilhet

Between Girga and Assiut, 2 June 1850
. . . I have seen Thebes; it's quite beautiful. We arrived one night at nine, in brilliant moonlight that flooded the columns. Dogs were barking, the great white ruins looked like ghosts, and the moon on the horizon, completely round and seeming to touch the earth, appeared to be motionless, resting there deliberately. Karnak gave us the impression of a life of giants. I spent a night at the feet of the colossus of Memnon, devoured by mosquitoes. The old scoundrel has a good face and is covered with inscriptions. Inscriptions and bird-droppings are the only two things in the ruins of Egypt that give any indication of life. The most worn stone doesn't grow a blade of grass; it falls into powder, like a mummy, and that is all . . . Often you see a tall, straight obelisk, with a long

white stain down its entire length, like a drapery
– wider at the top and tapering towards the base.
That is from the vultures, who have been coming
there to shit for centuries. It is a very handsome
effect and has a curious symbolism. It is as though
Nature said to the monuments of Egypt: 'You will
have none of me? You will not nourish the seed of
the lichen? *Eh bien, merde!'*

. . . At Esna I saw Kuchuk Hanem again; it was
sad. I found her changed. She had been sick. I shot
my bolt with her only once. The day was heavy
and overcast; her Abyssinian servant was sprinkling
water on the floor to cool the room. I stared at
her for a long while, so as to be able to keep a
picture of her in my mind. When I left, we told
her we would return the next day, but we did not.
However, I intensely relished the bitterness of it
all; that's the main thing, and I felt it in my very
bowels. At Kena I had a beautiful whore who
liked me very much and told me in sign language
that I had beautiful eyes. Her name is Hosna
et-Taouilah, which means 'the beautiful tall one';
and there was another, fat and lubricious, on top
of whom I enjoyed myself immensely and who
smelled of rancid butter.

I saw the Red Sea at Koseir. It was a journey
that took four days going and five for the return,
on camel-back and in a heat that in the middle of

the day rose to over 45 degrees Réaumur. That was a bit scorching: occasionally I longed for some beer, especially since our water smelled of sulphur and soap in addition to the taste of goat given it by the skins. We rose at three in the morning, and went to bed at nine at night, living on hard-boiled eggs, dry preserves, and watermelons. It was real desert life. All along the route we came upon the carcasses of camels that had died of exhaustion. There are places where you find great sheets of sand which seem to have been turned into a kind of paving, areas smooth and glazed like the threshing-floor of a barn: those are the places where camels stop to piss. With time the urine varnishes the sand and levels it like a floor. We had taken some cold meat with us, but in the middle of the second day had to abandon it. The odor of a leg of mutton we left on a stone immediately attracted a vulture, which began to fly round and round it.

We met great caravans of pilgrims going to Mecca (Koseir is the port where they take ship for Jidda, whence it is only three days to Mecca). Old Turks with their wives carried in baskets; a whole veiled harem called out to us like magpies as we passed; a dervish wearing a leopard-skin.

The camels in a caravan go sometimes one behind the other, sometimes all advancing on one broad front. When you see, foreshortened on the horizon, all those swaying heads coming toward you, it is like a horde of ostriches advancing slowly and gradually drawing together. At Koseir we saw pilgrims from the depths of Africa, poor negroes who have been on the march for a year, even two years. There are some curious sights. We also saw people from Bukhara, Tartars in pointed caps, who were preparing a meal in the shade of a shipwrecked boat made of red Indian wood. As for pearl-fishers, we saw only their canoes. Two men go in each canoe, one to row and one to dive, and they go out on to the open sea. When the diver returns to the surface he is bleeding from ears, nostrils, and eyes.

The day after my arrival I swam in the Red Sea. It was one of the most voluptuous pleasures of my life; I lolled in its waters as though I were lying on a thousand liquid breasts that were caressing my entire body.

That night Maxime, out of courtesy, and to honour his host, gave himself an attack of indigestion. We were lodged in a separate pavilion where we slept on divans and had a view of the sea; we were served by a young negro eunuch who had a very stylish way of carrying the tray of coffee-cups on his left arm. The morning we were to leave . . . I sat by myself, looking at the sea. Never will I forget that morning. I was stirred by it as though by an adventure; because of all the shells, shellfish, madrepores, corals, etc. the bottom of the sea is more brilliant than a spring meadow covered with primroses. As for the colour of the surface of the water, all possible tints passed through it, iridescent and melting together, from chocolate to amethyst, from pink to lapis lazuli and the palest green, and were I a painter I'd have been very embarrassed, thinking to what extent the reproduction of those real colours (admitting that were possible) would seem false.

We left Koseir that afternoon at four, very sadly. My eyes were wet when I embraced our host and climbed back on to my camel. It is always sad to leave a place to which one knows one will never return. Such are the *mélancolies du voyage*: perhaps they are one of the most rewarding things about travelling.

Flaubert to Louis Bouilhet

Cairo, 27 June [1850]

. . . Leaving our little boat was heart-rending. Back in the hotel here in Cairo my head was buzzing, as though after a long journey by stage-coach. The city seemed empty and silent, though in reality it was busy and full of people. The first night of my arrival here (last Tuesday) I kept hearing the soft sound of the oars in the water – that cadenced accompaniment to our long dreamy days for the past three months. The palm-trees here seemed to me so many brooms. I relived the entire trip, and in my heart I felt a bitter sweetness that was like the taste of a belch after good wine – when you say to yourself: 'Well, that was it.'

   . . . A bizarre psychological phenomenon! Back in Cairo (and since reading your good letter), I have been feeling myself bursting with intellectual intensity. The pot suddenly began to boil! I felt a burning need to write! I was wound up tight.

From Flaubert's Travel Notes

Monday, 1 July [1850]. *Last day* . . . Farewells . . . My sadness at leaving makes me realize what elation I must have felt on arrival. Women drawing water. Fellahin I shall never see again. A child bathing in the little canal of the *'Sakyeh*.

Sultan. The people around us prevent me from being sufficiently moved by his tears of gratitude; he wants to follow us to France! I had already experienced this emotion at Assuan; perhaps that is why it was so weak here.

Bulak. Hasanin. Farewells of the sailors. The real emotion was yesterday, when we embraced Raïs Ibrahim and said goodbye.

Our last night . . . Up until three in the morning . . . Dawn. Cocks crow, my two candles are lit. I am sweating, my eyes are burning. I have early morning chills. How many nights behind me! In four hours I leave Cairo. Farewell, Egypt! Allah! as the Arabs say.

Tuesday morning, 4.05 a.m.

Friday, 19 [July 1850]. [Alexandria.] Sail for Beirut on the *Alexandra* at seven in the morning. The boat left while I was asleep: I did not see the land of Egypt disappear on the horizon. I did not bid it my last farewells . . . Shall I ever return?

POCKET PENGUINS

1. Lady Chatterley's Trial
2. **Eric Schlosser** Cogs in the Great Machine
3. **Nick Hornby** Otherwise Pandemonium
4. **Albert Camus** Summer in Algiers
5. **P. D. James** Innocent House
6. **Richard Dawkins** The View from Mount Improbable
7. **India Knight** On Shopping
8. **Marian Keyes** Nothing Bad Ever Happens in Tiffany's
9. **Jorge Luis Borges** The Mirror of Ink
10. **Roald Dahl** A Taste of the Unexpected
11. **Jonathan Safran Foer** The Unabridged Pocketbook of Lightning
12. **Homer** The Cave of the Cyclops
13. **Paul Theroux** Two Stars
14. **Elizabeth David** Of Pageants and Picnics
15. **Anaïs Nin** Artists and Models
16. **Antony Beevor** Christmas at Stalingrad
17. **Gustave Flaubert** The Desert and the Dancing Girls
18. **Anne Frank** The Secret Annexe
19. **James Kelman** Where I Was
20. **Hari Kunzru** Noise
21. **Simon Schama** The Bastille Falls
22. **William Trevor** The Dressmaker's Child
23. **George Orwell** In Defence of English Cooking
24. **Michael Moore** Idiot Nation
25. **Helen Dunmore** Rose, 1944
26. **J. K. Galbraith** The Economics of Innocent Fraud
27. **Gervase Phinn** The School Inspector Calls
28. **W. G. Sebald** Young Austerlitz
29. **Redmond O'Hanlon** Borneo and the Poet
30. **Ali Smith** Ali Smith's Supersonic 70s
31. **Sigmund Freud** Forgetting Things
32. **Simon Armitage** King Arthur in the East Riding
33. **Hunter S. Thompson** Happy Birthday, Jack Nicholson
34. **Vladimir Nabokov** Cloud, Castle, Lake
35. **Niall Ferguson** 1914: Why the World Went to War

POCKET PENGUINS